Heavens' Embroidered Cloths

Poems by W. B. Yeats

Jack Butler Yeats THE BOATMAN OF THE LAKE

HEAVENS' EMBROIDERED CLOTHS

Poems by W. B. Yeats

SELECTED AND WITH AN INTRODUCTION BY PAMELA TODD

PAVILION

FOR DAVID, AS ALWAYS

First published in Great Britain in 1996 by
PAVILION BOOKS LIMITED
26 Upper Ground, London SE1 9PD

A CIP catalogue record for this book is available from the British Library

ISBN 1 85793 654 X

Designed by David Fordham
Typeset in Helvetica Bold and Garamond Light by SX Composing Ltd, Rayleigh
Printed and bound in Italy by Graphicom

2 4 6 8 10 9 7 5 3 1

This book may be ordered by post direct from the publisher.
Please contact the Marketing Department. But try your bookshop first.

Contents

Jack Butler Yeats   HIGH SPRING TIDE, ROSSES POINT

HEAVENS' EMBROIDERED CLOTHS

'THERE ARE SOME POETS,' WROTE T.S. ELIOT ON THE DEATH OF W.B. YEATS IN 1939, 'WHOSE poetry can be considered more or less in isolation, for experience and delight. There are others whose poetry, though giving equally experience and delight, has a larger historical importance. Yeats was one of the latter: he was one of those few whose history is the history of their own time, who are a part of the consciousness of an age which cannot be understood without them. This is a very high position to assign to him: but I believe that it is one which is secure.'

In our own time Yeats's greatness is universally acknowledged. J.B. Priestley called him 'a poet first, last, and all the time. Not only a great poet but probably the greatest poet of this century'. We turn to him today for the force and charm of his work, the intensity of his poetic vision and the astonishing power of his imagination. Most poets, even the finest, have a golden period, but Yeats was rare in his ability to keep writing good poems throughout a long career which straddled two centuries.

He is a deeply personal poet. From the outset he believed that a poet's primary duty was 'to look into that little faltering flame that one calls oneself' and to put into poetry 'the emotions and experiences' that have been most important to him in his life. 'We should write out our thoughts,' he said, 'in as nearly as possible the language we thought them in, as though in a letter to an intimate friend. We should not disguise them in any way; for our lives give them force as the lives of people in plays give force to their words.'

Accordingly, we find everywhere in his poems the passions and personalities that shaped his life. His love of Ireland runs like a deep current through his work. He used the popular forms of the people – balladry, folk-song and Celtic myth and legends – but tilted them into strangeness, beauty and mystery. His frustrated love for Maud Gonne served as a poetic impulse, as did the serenity he eventually found in his late marriage to Georgina Hyde-Lees. His lifelong obsession with magic and mysticism – he was a follower of Madame Blavatsky and joined the Hermetic Order of the Golden Dawn in 1890 – was a source of concern to his family, but Yeats defended it as 'the business of my life' and 'next to my poetry, the most important pursuit of my life'.

Certainly his interest never wavered throughout his life and, although it is sometimes challenging for the reader to penetrate, it supplied the young Yeats with a store of symbols and images that he could call on for the rest of his life. These symbols are drawn largely from the world of nature – tree, sea, rose, sun and moon (as well as tower, house and mask) – and recur throughout his poems, detonating into images that evoke rather than describe. His use of bird imagery, especially lonely birds like the heron, hawk, eagle and swan, often depicted floating alone upon the wind or alighting upon a lake or river, is very marked. Yeats thought of himself as 'the last of the romantics', a man born out of his time, but as his work develops he becomes also the first of the moderns.

His early training as a painter shines through in the pictorial quality of his poems, but their meaning is shifting, mysterious, complicated by his own emotions, coloured by his own life. This is deliberate. In his introduction to *Poems*, published by T. Fisher Unwin in 1908, he wrote: 'I must leave my myths and symbols to explain themselves as the years go by and one poem lights up another . . .' And extraordinarily this is what they do. The last poems illuminate some of his earliest imagery. He was ever alive to the mystery of his work and careful not to limit the reader's imaginative response by fixing any of his poems with too specific a meaning. In 1935 he politely declined to comment on a poem that Maurice Wollman wanted to include in his anthology, *Modern Poetry*, explaining that 'if an author interprets a poem of his own he limits its suggestibility'. This was crucial. Yeats attracts us still because the success of his poems lies in the joint achievement of the poet and the reader.

Yeats was born into an artistic, middle-class, Protestant family on 13 June 1865 in Dublin. His father, John, was a painter and his younger brother, Jack, went on to become an artist of striking talent. 'Willie', the eldest of four, was a dreamy youth, tutored at home until, in 1877, he was sent to the Godolphin School in Hammersmith. Formal education he found a reductive, rather than enlarging, experience. It left him no time for reverie and he did not distinguish himself. (His spelling remained appalling all his life.) The family lived in London for that was where his father's work was conducted, but the children holidayed in their beloved Sligo, where, at fifteen, the awakening of sex came upon Yeats 'like the bursting of a shell'. He began to dramatize himself as a magician and poet. When Katharine Tynan first met him in 1885 he seemed to her 'all dreams and all gentleness'.

His father encouraged him to register at the Metropolitan School of Art in Dublin, but he was not cut out to be a painter. He had been composing poetry for two years, and whilst at art school in 1885 his first lyrics were published in the March issue of *Dublin University Review*. The following year he abandoned his art studies in favour of a career as a professional writer. He came to London but felt shy, insignificant and out of place. Friendship sustained him. Yeats once wrote that 'Friendship is all the house I have', and in his life he forged deep and lasting attachments to people.

He was always generous and loyal. To Ezra Pound he gave $200 from a literary award he had just won himself; he helped James Joyce when he was living in poverty in Switzerland and T.S. Eliot, twenty-three years his junior, felt that he always 'offered terms of equality, as to a fellow worker, a practitioner of the same mystery'. Women undoubtedly found him attractive. Katharine Tynan describes his 'dark face, its touch of vivid colouring, the night-black hair, the eager eyes' and photographs of him young and old prove him to be a figure of brooding elegance and style, with his flowing hair (raven-black when young; snow-white but still full when old), his black cape and wide tie knotted in a large loose bow.

When he was twenty-three he met the woman who would dominate his life and his poetry – the intense, fervent, passionate, revolutionary beauty, Maud Gonne. Yeats was immediately smitten, lost. He had never seen in a 'living woman, so great beauty' and she was for him a goddess, 'a Helen' a 'Pallas Athene'. 'Her complexion,' he wrote, 'was luminous, like that of apple blossom through which the light falls, and I remember her standing that first day by a great heap of such blossoms in the window'. She praised his poetry and encouraged him to deploy it as part of the struggle for an independent Irish nation.

'Did I tell you,' he wrote four days after this meeting to Ellen O'Leary, 'how much I admire Miss Gonne? She will make many converts to her political belief. If she said the world was flat or the moon an old caubeen tossed up into the sky I would be proud to be of her party'.

His long, unsuccessful courtship of her pervades his poetry. He proposed often, first in 1891 and last in 1917, when the death of her husband, the Irish revolutionary hero John MacBride, in the Easter Rising of 1916, had made her once more free. She refused him every time. He even proposed to her daughter, Iseult, who, though flattered, also refused. She strides, haughty, flamboyant, statuesque (she was six feet tall) through poems like 'Love's Loneliness', 'The Pity of Love', 'The Sorrow of Love', 'No Second Troy' and the cautionary 'O Do Not Love too Long' – celebrated, idealized and berated for tormenting him and consuming so much of his life. His journal entry for 22 January 1909 reads:

> How much of the best I have done and still do is but the attempt to explain myself to her? If she understood, I should lack a reason for writing, and one never can have too many reasons for doing what is so laborious.

The crafting of his poems was, for Yeats, a laborious task of long practice, and long experiment. He wrote a great deal at Coole Park, the home of Lady Augusta Gregory, and she recalled how Yeats's 'mutterings' would go on for hours with no more than a line of poetry to show for it. His great friendship with Lady Gregory led to the setting up in December 1904 of the Abbey Theatre, where he produced and championed young Irish playwrights like J.M. Synge, whose dazzling *Playboy of the Western World* he defended in the teeth of riots outside the theatre, and Sean O'Casey.

In 1917 when both Maud and her daughter Iseult had rejected his proposals he asked a third woman – Georgina Hyde-Lees – and she accepted. He was fifty-two, an age when many poets are producing little that is new and exciting, but marriage rejuvenated him and prompted some of his most exciting work.

The couple eventually moved into Thoor Ballylee, an old Norman tower on Lady Gregory's estate, which Yeats had bought along with two thatched cottages for £35. The restoration work was long, expensive and interrupted by the political turmoil of the time but the place was important to him, it linked him to the Irish past and he saw it as 'a setting for my old age, a place to influence lawless youth, with its severity and antiquity'.

With the serenity of his marriage, the pleasures of late fatherhood, and the dramatically exciting discovery of his wife's ability to produce automatic writing, came a new burst of intellectual energy and in his poetry a new simplicity, restraint and tautness. Fame came too. Queen's University, Belfast gave him an honorary degree in July 1922 and Trinity College in Dublin another in December. He was made a Senator of the newly formed Free State for his services to Ireland and in 1923 he was awarded the Nobel Prize for Literature.

In his sixties he was asked by a doctor, who was treating him for high blood-pressure, if he had had any over-excitement of late. 'I have lived a life of excitement,' he loftily replied. He died in France in 1939 aged seventy-four.

PAMELA TODD 1996

THE WOODS OF ARCADY ARE DEAD,

And over is their antique joy;

Of old the world on dreaming fed;

Grey Truth is now her painted toy;

Yet still she turns her restless head;

But O, sick children of the world,

Of all the many changing things

In dreary dancing past us whirled,

To the cracked tune that Chronos sings,

Words alone are certain good.

Where are now the warring kings,

Word be-mockers? – By the Rood

Where are now the warring kings?

An idle word is now their glory,

By the stammering schoolboy said,

Reading some entangled story:

The kings of the old time are dead;

The wandering earth herself may be

Only a sudden flaming word,

In clanging space a moment heard,

Troubling the endless reverie.

Then nowise worship dusty deeds,

Nor seek, for this is also sooth,

To hunger fiercely after truth,

Lest all thy toiling only breeds

New dreams, new dreams; there is no truth

Saving in thine own heart. Seek, then,

No learning from the starry men,

Who follow with the optic glass

The whirling ways of stars that pass –

Seek, then, for this is also sooth,

No word of theirs – the cold star-bane

Has cloven and rent their hearts in twain,

And dead is all their human truth.

Go gather by the humming sea

Some twisted, echo-harbouring shell,

And to its lips thy story tell,

And they thy comforters will be,

Rewording in melodious guile

Thy fretful words a little while,

Till they shall singing fade in ruth

And die a pearly brotherhood;

Nathaniel Hone, the Younger   A View of Glenmalure, with a Shepherd and Flock

For words alone are certain good:
Sing, then, for this is also sooth.

I must be gone: there is a grave
Where daffodil and lily wave,
And I would please the hapless faun,
Buried under the sleepy ground,
With mirthful songs before the dawn.
His shouting days with mirth were crowned;

And still I dream he treads the lawn,
Walking ghostly on the dew,
Pierced by my glad singing through,
My songs of old earth's dreamy youth:
But ah! she dreams not now; dream thou!
For fair are poppies on the brow:
Dream, dream, for this is also sooth.

THERE WAS A MAN WHOM SORROW NAMED HIS FRIEND,

And he, of his high comrade Sorrow dreaming,
Went walking with slow steps along the gleaming
And humming sands, where windy surges wend:
And he called loudly to the stars to bend
From their pale thrones and comfort him, but they
Among themselves laugh on and sing alway:
And then the man whom Sorrow named his friend
Cried out, *Dim sea, hear my most piteous story!*
The sea swept on and cried her old cry still,
Rolling along in dreams from hill to hill.
He fled the persecution of her glory
And, in a far-off, gentle valley stopping,
Cried all his story to the dewdrops glistening.
But naught they heard, for they are always listening,
The dewdrops, for the sound of their own dropping.

And then the man whom Sorrow named his friend
Sought once again the shore, and found a shell,
And thought, *I will my heavy story tell*
Till my own words, re-echoing, shall send
Their sadness through a hollow, pearly heart;
And my own tale again for me shall sing,
And my own whispering words be comforting,
And lo! my ancient burden may depart.
Then he sang softly nigh the pearly rim;
But the sad dweller by the sea-ways lone
Changed all he sang to inarticulate moan
Among her wildering whirls, forgetting him.

15

Frederick William Newton Whitehead   THE HAUNT OF THE MOORHEN

I PASSED ALONG THE WATER'S EDGE BELOW THE HUMID TREES,
My spirit rocked in evening light, the rushes round my knees,
My spirit rocked in sleep and sighs; and saw the moorfowl pace
All dripping on a grassy slope, and saw them cease to chase
Each other round in circles, and heard the eldest speak:
Who holds the world between His bill and made us strong or weak
Is an undying moorfowl, and He lives beyond the sky.
The rains are from His dripping wing, the moonbeams from His eye.
I passed a little further on and heard a lotus talk:
Who made the world and ruleth it, He hangeth on a stalk,
For I am in His image made, and all this tinkling tide
Is but a sliding drop of rain between His petals wide.
A little way within the gloom a roebuck raised his eyes
Brimful of starlight, and he said: *The Stamper of the Skies,*
He is a gentle roebuck; for how else, I pray, could He
Conceive a thing so sad and soft, a gentle thing like me?
I passed a little further on and heard a peacock say:
Who made the grass and made the worms and made my feathers gay,
He is a monstrous peacock, and He waveth all the night
His languid tail above us, lit with myriad spots of light.

AUTUMN IS OVER THE LONG LEAVES THAT LOVE US

And over the mice in the barley sheaves;
Yellow the leaves of the rowan above us,
And yellow the wet wild-strawberry leaves.

The hour of the waning of love has beset us,
And weary and worn are our sad souls now;
Let us part, ere the season of passion forget us,
With a kiss and a tear on thy drooping brow.

Walter Frederick Osborne
'WHEN YELLOW LEAVES OR NONE SO FEW HANG UPON THOSE BOUGHS THAT SHAKE AGAINST THE COLD'

Edward Wilkins Waite   An Autumn Day

'**Y**OUR EYES THAT ONCE WERE NEVER

WEARY OF MINE

Are bowed in sorrow under pendulous lids,
Because our love is waning.'
                                        And then she:
'Although our love is waning, let us stand
By the lone border of the lake once more,
Together in that hour of gentleness
When the poor tired child, Passion, falls asleep.
How far away the stars seem, and how far
Is our first kiss, and ah, how old my heart!'
Pensive they paced along the faded leaves,
While slowly he whose hand held hers replied:
'Passion has often worn our wandering hearts.'

The woods were round them, and the yellow leaves
Fell like faint meteors in the gloom, and once
A rabbit old and lame limped down the path;
Autumn was over him: and now they stood
On the lone border of the lake once more:

Turning, he saw that she had thrust dead leaves
Gathered in silence, dewy as her eyes,
In bosom and hair.
                                'Ah, do not mourn,' he said,
'That we are tired, for other loves await us;
Hate on and love through unrepining hours.
Before us lies eternity; our souls
Are love, and a continual farewell.'

THE STOLEN CHILD

WHERE DIPS THE ROCKY HIGHLAND
Of Sleuth Wood in the lake,
There lies a leafy island
Where flapping herons wake
The drowsy water-rats;
There we've hid our faery vats,
Full of berries
And of reddest stolen cherries.
Come away, O human child!
To the waters and the wild
With a faery, hand in hand,
For the world's more full of weeping
  than you can understand.

We foot it all the night,
Weaving olden dances,
Mingling hands and mingling glances
Till the moon has taken flight;
To and fro we leap
And chase the frothy bubbles,
While the world is full of troubles
And is anxious in its sleep.
Come away, O human child!
To the waters and the wild
With a faery, hand in hand,
For the world's more full of weeping
  than you can understand.

Where the wave of moonlight glosses
The dim grey sands with light,
Far off by furthest Rosses

Where the wandering water gushes
From the hills above Glen-Car,
In pools among the rushes

Walter Frederick Osborne   A GLADE IN THE PHOENIX PARK

That scarce could bathe a star,
We seek for slumbering trout
And whispering in their ears
Give them unquiet dreams;
Leaning softly out
From ferns that drop their tears
Over the young streams.
Come away, O human child!
To the waters and the wild
With a faery, hand in hand,
For the world's more full of weeping
  than you can understand.

Away with us he's going,
The solemn-eyed:
He'll hear no more the lowing
Of the calves on the warm hillside
Or the kettle on the hob
Sing peace into his breast,
Or see the brown mice bob
Round and round the oatmeal-chest.
For he comes, the human child
To the waters and the wild
With a faery, hand in hand,
From a world more full of weeping
  than he can understand.

D OWN BY THE SALLEY GARDENS MY LOVE AND I DID MEET;

She passed the salley gardens with little snow-white feet.

She bid me take love easy, as the leaves grow on the tree;

But I, being young and foolish, with her would not agree.

In a field by the river my love and I did stand,

And on my leaning shoulder she laid her snow-white hand.

She bid me take life easy, as the grass grows on the weirs;

But I was young and foolish, and now am full of tears.

YOU WAVES, THOUGH YOU DANCE BY MY FEET LIKE CHILDREN AT PLAY,

Though you glow and you glance, though you purr and you dart;

In the Junes that were warmer than these are, the waves were more gay,

When I was a boy with never a crack in my heart.

The herring are not in the tides as they were of old;

My sorrow! for many a creak gave the creel in the cart

That carried the take to Sligo town to be sold,

When I was a boy with never a crack in my heart.

And ah, you proud maiden, you are not so fair when his oar

Is heard on the water, as they were, the proud and apart,

Who paced in the eve by the nets on the pebbly shore,

When I was a boy with never a crack in my heart.

William Henry Bartlett   CLEANING THE NETS, CO. DONEGAL

I WILL ARISE AND GO NOW, AND GO TO INNISFREE,
And a small cabin build there, of clay and wattles made:
Nine bean-rows will I have there, a hive for the honey-bee,
And live alone in the bee-loud glade.

And I shall have some peace there, for peace comes dropping slow,
Dropping from the veils of the morning to where the cricket sings;
There midnight's all a glimmer, and noon a purple glow,
And evening full of the linnet's wings.

I will arise and go now, for always night and day
I hear lake water lapping with low sounds by the shore;
While I stand on the roadway, or on the pavements grey,
I hear it in the deep heart's core.

Paul Henry LAKESIDE COTTAGES

THE BRAWLING OF A SPARROW IN THE EAVES,

The brilliant moon and all the milky sky,

And all that famous harmony of leaves,

Had blotted out man's image and his cry.

A girl arose that had red mournful lips

And seemed the greatness of the world in tears,

Doomed like Odysseus and the labouring ships

And proud as Priam murdered with his peers;

Arose, and on the instant clamorous eaves,

A climbing moon upon an empty sky,

And all that lamentation of the leaves,

Could but compose man's image and his cry.

THE PITY OF LOVE

A PITY BEYOND ALL TELLING

Is hid in the heart of love:

The folk who are buying and selling,

The clouds on their journey above,

The cold wet winds ever blowing,

And the shadowy hazel grove

Where mouse-grey waters are flowing,

Threaten the head that I love.

Sir William Orpen   IN DUBLIN BAY, 1909

31

*R*ED ROSE, PROUD ROSE, SAD ROSE
    OF ALL MY DAYS!

Come near me, while I sing the ancient ways:
Cuchulain battling with the bitter tide;
The Druid, grey, wood-nurtured, quiet-eyed,
Who cast round Fergus dreams, and ruin untold;
And thine own sadness, whereof stars, grown old
In dancing silver-sandalled on the sea,
Sing in their high and lonely melody.
Come near, that no more blinded by man's fate,
I find under the boughs of love and hate,
In all poor foolish things that live a day,
Eternal beauty wandering on her way.

Come near, come near, come near – Ah, leave me still
A little space for the rose-breath to fill!
Lest I no more hear common things that crave;
The weak worm hiding down in its small cave,
The field-mouse running by me in the grass,
And heavy mortal hopes that toil and pass;
But seek alone to hear the strange things said
By God to the bright hearts of those long dead,
And learn to chaunt a tongue men do not know.
Come near; I would, before my time to go,
Sing of old Eire and the ancient ways:
Red Rose, proud Rose, sad Rose of all my days.

WHEN YOU ARE OLD AND GREY AND FULL OF SLEEP,

And nodding by the fire, take down this book,

And slowly read, and dream of the soft look

Your eyes had once, and of their shadows deep;

How many loved your moments of glad grace,

And loved your beauty with love false or true,

But one man loved the pilgrim soul in you,

And loved the sorrows of your changing face;

And bending down beside the glowing bars,

Murmur, a little sadly, how Love fled

And paced upon the mountains overhead

And hid his face amid a crowd of stars.

I WOULD THAT WE WERE, MY BELOVED, WHITE BIRDS ON THE FOAM OF THE SEA!

We tire of the flame of the meteor, before it can fade and flee;

And the flame of the blue star of twilight, hung low on the rim of the sky,

Has awaked in our hearts, my beloved, a sadness that may not die.

A weariness comes from those dreamers, dew-dabbled, the lily and rose;

Ah, dream not of them, my beloved, the flame of the meteor that goes,

Or the flame of the blue star that lingers hung low in the fall of the dew:

For I would we were changed to white birds on the wandering foam: I and you!

I am haunted by numberless islands, and many a Danaan shore,

Where Time would surely forget us, and Sorrow come near us no more;

Soon far from the rose and the lily and fret of the flames would we be,

Were we only white birds, my beloved, buoyed out on the foam of the sea!

Peter Graham   SEA-GIRT CRAGS, 1886

William Turner (of Oxford) THE DAWN

A DREAM OF DEATH

I DREAMED THAT ONE HAD DIED
   IN A STRANGE PLACE

Near no accustomed hand;
And they had nailed the boards above her face,
The peasants of that land,
Wondering to lay her in that solitude,
And raised above her mound
A cross they had made out of two bits of wood,
And planted cypress round;
And left her to the indifferent stars above
Until I carved these words:
She was more beautiful than thy first love,
But now lies under boards.

WHO GOES WITH FERGUS?

WHO WILL GO DRIVE WITH FERGUS NOW,
And pierce the deep wood's woven shade,
And dance upon the level shore?
Young man, lift up your russet brow,
And lift your tender eyelids, maid,
And brood on hopes and fear no more.

And no more turn aside and brood
Upon love's bitter mystery;
For Fergus rules the brazen cars,
And rules the shadows of the wood,
And the white breast of the dim sea
And all dishevelled wandering stars.

BELOVED, GAZE IN THINE OWN HEART,

The holy tree is growing there;

From joy the holy branches start,

And all the trembling flowers they bear.

The changing colours of its fruit

Have dowered the stars with merry light;

The surety of its hidden root

Has planted quiet in the night;

The shaking of its leafy head

Has given the waves their melody,

And made my lips and music wed,

Murmuring a wizard song for thee.

There the Loves a circle go,

The flaming circle of our days,

Gyring, spiring to and fro

In those great ignorant leafy ways;

Remembering all that shaken hair

And how the wingèd sandals dart,

Thine eyes grow full of tender care:

Beloved, gaze in thine own heart.

Gaze no more in the bitter glass

The demons, with their subtle guile,

Lift up before us when they pass,

Or only gaze a little while;

For there a fatal image grows

That the stormy night receives,

Roots half hidden under snows,

Broken boughs and blackened leaves.

For all things turn to barrenness

In the dim glass the demons hold,

The glass of outer weariness,

Made when God slept in times of old.

There, through the broken branches, go

The ravens of unresting thought;

Flying, crying, to and fro,

Cruel claw and hungry throat,

Or else they stand and sniff the wind,

And shake their ragged wings; alas!

Thy tender eyes grow all unkind:

Gaze no more in the bitter glass.

Edward Wilkins Waite   MISTY MORNING

ALL THINGS UNCOMELY AND BROKEN, ALL THINGS WORN OUT AND OLD,

The cry of a child by the roadway, the creak of a lumbering cart,

The heavy steps of the ploughman, splashing the wintry mould,

Are wronging your image that blossoms a rose in the deeps of my heart.

The wrong of unshapely things is a wrong too great to be told;

I hunger to build them anew and sit on a green knoll apart,

With the earth and the sky and the water, re-made, like a casket of gold

For my dreams of your image that blossoms a rose in the deeps of my heart.

Frederick William Burton   ANNIE CALLWELL.

THE FISH

ALTHOUGH YOU HIDE IN THE EBB AND FLOW

Of the pale tide when the moon has set,

The people of coming days will know

About the casting out of my net,

And how you have leaped times out of mind

Over the little silver cords,

And think that you were hard and unkind,

And blame you with many bitter words.

HE REPROVES THE CURLEW

O CURLEW, CRY NO MORE IN THE AIR,

Or only to the water in the West;

Because your crying brings to my mind

Passion-dimmed eyes and long heavy hair

That was shaken out over my breast:

There is enough evil in the crying of wind.

THE VALLEY OF THE BLACK PIG

THE DEWS DROP SLOWLY AND DREAMS GATHER: UNKNOWN SPEARS

Suddenly hurtle before my dream-awakened eyes,

And then the clash of fallen horsemen and the cries

Of unknown perishing armies beat about my ears.

We who still labour by the cromlech on the shore,

The grey cairn on the hill, when day sinks drowned in dew,

Being weary of the world's empires, bow down to you,

Master of the still stars and of the flaming door.

Walter Frederick Osborne   An October Morning

THE JESTER WALKED IN THE GARDEN:
The garden had fallen still;
He bade his soul rise upward
And stand on her window-sill.

It rose in a straight blue garment,
When owls began to call:
It had grown wise-tongued by thinking
Of a quiet and light footfall;

But the young queen would not listen;
She rose in her pale night-gown;
She drew in the heavy casement
And pushed the latches down.

He bade his heart go to her,
When the owls called out no more;
In a red and quivering garment
It sang to her through the door.

It had grown sweet-tongued by dreaming
Of a flutter of flower-like hair;
But she took up her fan from the table
And waved it off on the air.

'I have cap and bells,' he pondered,
'I will send them to her and die';
And when the morning whitened
He left them where she went by.

She laid them upon her bosom,
Under a cloud of her hair,
And her red lips sang them a love-song
Till stars grew out of the air.

She opened her door and her window,
And the heart and the soul came through,
To her right hand came the red one,
To her left hand came the blue.

They set up a noise like crickets,
A chattering wise and sweet,
And her hair was a folded flower
And the quiet of love in her feet.

Mildred Anne Butler   A BYPATH

I WANDER BY THE EDGE

Of this desolate lake

Where wind cries in the sedge:

Until the axle break

That keeps the stars in their round,

And hands hurl in the deep

The banners of East and West,

And the girdle of light is unbound,

Your breast will not lie by the breast

Of your beloved in sleep.

He THINKS OF HIS PAST GREATNESS
WHEN A PART OF THE CONSTELLATIONS
OF HEAVEN

I HAVE DRUNK ALE FROM THE COUNTRY
OF THE YOUNG

And weep because I know all things now:

I have been a hazel-tree, and they hung

The Pilot Star and the Crooked Plough

Among my leaves in times out of mind:

I became a rush that horses tread:

I became a man, a hater of the wind,

Knowing one, out of all things, alone, that his head

May not lie on the breast nor his lips on the hair

Of the woman that he loves, until he dies.

O beast of the wilderness, bird of the air,

Must I endure your amorous cries?

William Percy French   IN THE WEST 1914

47

William Mulready   THE MOOR AT SUNRISE

HAD I THE HEAVENS' EMBROIDERED CLOTHS,

Enwrought with golden and silver light,

The blue and the dim and the dark cloths

Of night and light and the half-light,

I would spread the cloths under your feet:

But I, being poor, have only my dreams;

I have spread my dreams under your feet;

Tread softly because you tread on my dreams.

HE TELLS OF A VALLEY FULL OF LOVERS

I DREAMED THAT I STOOD IN A VALLEY, AND AMID SIGHS,

For happy lovers passed two by two where I stood;

And I dreamed my lost love came stealthily out of the wood

With her cloud-pale eyelids falling on dream-dimmed eyes:

I cried in my dream, *O women, bid the young men lay*

Their heads on your knees, and drown their eyes with your hair,

Or remembering hers they will find no other face fair

Till all the valleys of the world have been withered away.

I HAVE HEARD THE PIGEONS OF THE SEVEN WOODS

Make their faint thunder, and the garden bees

Hum in the lime-tree flowers; and put away

The unavailing outcries and the old bitterness

That empty the heart. I have forgot awhile

Tara uprooted, and new commonness

Upon the throne and crying about the streets

And hanging its paper flowers from post to post,

Because it is alone of all things happy.

I am contented, for I know that Quiet

Wanders laughing and eating her wild heart

Among pigeons and bees, while that Great Archer,

Who but awaits His hour to shoot, still hangs

A cloudy quiver over Pairc-na-lee.

Ernest Parton   IN A FAIRY WOODLAND

THE WITHERING
OF THE BOUGHS

I CRIED WHEN THE MOON WAS MURMURING TO THE BIRDS:
'Let peewit call and curlew cry where they will,
I long for your merry and tender and pitiful words,
For the roads are unending, and there is no place to my mind.'
The honey-pale moon lay low on the sleepy hill,
And I fell asleep upon lonely Echtge of streams.
No boughs have withered because of the wintry wind;
The boughs have withered because I have told them my dreams.

I know of the leafy paths that the witches take
Who come with their crowns of pearl and their spindles of wool,
And their secret smile, out of the depths of the lake;
I know where a dim moon drifts, where the Danaan kind
Wind and unwind their dancing when the light grows cool
On the island lawns, their feet where the pale foam gleams.
No boughs have withered because of the wintry wind;
The boughs have withered because I have told them my dreams.

I know of the sleepy country, where swans fly round
Coupled with golden chains, and sing as they fly.
A king and a queen are wandering there, and the sound
Has made them so happy and hopeless, so deaf and so blind
With wisdom, they wander till all the years have gone by;
I know, and the curlew and peewit on Echtge of streams.
No boughs have withered because of the wintry wind;
The boughs have withered because I have told them my dreams.

Mildred Anne Butler SHADES OF EVENING

53

O DO NOT LOVE TOO LONG

SWEETHEART, DO NOT LOVE TOO LONG:

I loved long and long,
And grew to be out of fashion
Like an old song.

All through the years of our youth
Neither could have known
Their own thought from the other's,
We were so much at one.

But O, in a minute she changed –
O do not love too long,
Or you will grow out of fashion
Like an old song.

THE RAGGED WOOD

O HURRY WHERE BY WATER AMONG THE TREES

The delicate-stepping stag and his lady sigh,
When they have but looked upon their images –
Would none had ever loved but you and I!

Or have you heard that sliding silver-shoed
Pale silver-proud queen-woman of the sky,
When the sun looked out of his golden hood? –
O that none ever loved but you and I!

O hurry to the ragged wood, for there
I will drive all those lovers out and cry –
O my share of the world, O yellow hair!
No one has ever loved but you and I.

Henry William Banks Davis TOWARDS EVENING IN THE FOREST

THE COMING OF WIDSOM WITH TIME

THOUGH LEAVES ARE MANY, THE ROOT IS ONE;
Through all the lying days of my youth
I swayed my leaves and flowers in the sun;
Now I may wither into the truth.

Frederick William Burton A Connemara Peasant Girl

BROWN PENNY

I WHISPERED, 'I AM TOO YOUNG,'
And then, 'I am old enough';
Wherefore I threw a penny
To find out if I might love.
'Go and love, go and love, young man,
If the lady be young and fair.'
Ah, penny, brown penny, brown penny,
I am looped in the loops of her hair.

O love is the crooked thing,
There is nobody wise enough
To find out all that is in it,
For he would be thinking of love
Till the stars had run away
And the shadows eaten the moon.
Ah, penny, brown penny, brown penny.
One cannot begin it too soon.

Mildred Anne Butler   PEACOCKS IN A FIELD

WHAT'S RICHES TO HIM

That has made a great peacock
With the pride of his eye?
The wind-beaten, stone-grey,
And desolate Three Rock
Would nourish his whim.
Live he or die
Amid wet rocks and heather,
His ghost will be gay
Adding feather to feather
For the pride of his eye.

SUDDENLY I SAW THE COLD AND ROOK-DELIGHTING HEAVEN

That seemed as though ice burned and was but the more ice,

And thereupon imagination and heart were driven

So wild that every casual thought of that and this

Vanished, and left but memories, that should be out of season

With the hot blood of youth, of love crossed long ago;

And I took all the blame out of all sense and reason,

Until I cried and trembled and rocked to and fro,

Riddled with light. Ah! when the ghost begins to quicken,

Confusion of the death-bed over, is it sent

Out naked on the roads, as the books say, and stricken

By the injustice of the skies for punishment?

Albert Goodwin   NIGHTFALL

61

Edward R. Taylor THE LILY POND

THE WILD SWANS AT COOLE

THE TREES ARE IN THEIR AUTUMN BEAUTY,
The woodland paths are dry,
Under the October twilight the water
Mirrors a still sky;
Upon the brimming water among the stones
Are nine-and-fifty swans.

The nineteenth autumn has come upon me
Since I first made my count;
I saw, before I had well finished,
All suddenly mount
And scatter wheeling in great broken rings
Upon their clamorous wings.

I have looked upon those brilliant creatures,
And now my heart is sore.
All's changed since I, hearing at twilight,
The first time on this shore,
The bell-beat of their wings above my head,
Trod with a lighted tread.

Unwearied still, lover by lover,
They paddle in the cold
Companionable streams or climb the air;
Their hearts have not grown old;
Passion or conquest, wander where they will,
Attend upon them still.

But now they drift on the still water,
Mysterious, beautiful;
Among what rushes will they build,
By what lake's edge or pool
Delight men's eyes when I awake some day
To find they have flown away?

THE COLLAR-BONE OF A HARE

WOULD I COULD CAST A SAIL ON THE WATER
Where many a king has gone
And many a king's daughter,
And alight at the comely trees and the lawn,
The playing upon pipes and the dancing,
And learn that the best thing is
To change my loves while dancing
And pay but a kiss for a kiss.

I would find by the edge of that water
The collar-bone of a hare
Worn thin by the lapping of water,
And pierce it through with a gimlet, and stare
At the old bitter world where they marry in churches,
And laugh over the untroubled water
At all who marry in churches,
Through the white thin bone of a hare.

MEMORY

ONE HAD A LOVELY FACE,
And two or three had charm,
But charm and face were in vain
Because the mountain grass
Cannot but keep the form
Where the mountain hare has lain.

George Stevens   A Hare Sitting

Benjamin William Leader   STREAM IN SUMMERTIME

ALTHOUGH I CAN SEE HIM STILL,

The freckled man who goes

To a grey place on a hill

In grey Connemara clothes

At dawn to cast his flies,

It's long since I began

To call up to the eyes

This wise and simple man.

All day I'd looked in the face

What I had hoped 'twould be

To write for my own race

And the reality;

The living men that I hate,

The dead man that I loved,

The craven man in his seat,

The insolent unreproved,

And no knave brought to book

Who has won a drunken cheer,

The witty man and his joke

Aimed at the commonest ear,

The clever man who cries

The catch-cries of the clown,

The beating down of the wise

And great Art beaten down.

Maybe a twelvemonth since

Suddenly I began,

In scorn of this audience,

Imagining a man,

And his sun-freckled face,

And grey Connemara cloth,

Climbing up to a place

Where stone is dark under froth,

And the down-turn of his wrist

When the flies drop in the stream;

A man who does not exist,

A man who is but a dream;

And cried, 'Before I am old

I shall have written him one

Poem maybe as cold

And passionate as the dawn.

THE HAWK

'CALL DOWN THE HAWK FROM THE AIR;
Let him be hooded or caged
Till the yellow eye has grown mild,
For larder and spit are bare,
The old cook enraged,
The scullion gone wild.'

'I will not be clapped in a hood,
Nor a cage, nor alight upon wrist,
Now I have learnt to be proud
Hovering over the wood
In the broken mist
Or tumbling cloud.'

'What tumbling cloud did you cleave,
Yellow-eyed hawk of the mind,
Last evening? that I, who had sat
Dumbfounded before a knave,
Should give to my friend
A pretence of wit.'

TO A SQUIRREL AT KYLE-NA-NO

COME PLAY WITH ME;
Why should you run
Through the shaking tree
As though I'd a gun
To strike you dead?
When all I would do
Is to scratch your head
And let you go.

Robert Collinson   Squirrels in a Wood

THE CAT WENT HERE AND THERE
And the moon spun round like a top,
And the nearest kin of the moon,
The creeping cat, looked up.
Black Minnaloushe stared at the moon,
For, wander and wail as he would,
The pure cold light in the sky
Troubled his animal blood.
Minnaloushe runs in the grass
Lifting his delicate feet.
Do you dance, Minnaloushe, do you dance?
When two close kindred meet,
What better than call a dance?
Maybe the moon may learn,

Tired of that courtly fashion,
A new dance turn.
Minnaloushe creeps through the grass
From moonlit place to place,
The sacred moon overhead
Has taken a new phase.
Does Minnaloushe know that his pupils
Will pass from change to change,
And that from round to crescent,
From crescent to round they range?
Minnaloushe creeps through the grass
Alone, important and wise,
And lifts to the changing moon
His changing eyes.

William Fraser Garden   THE WOOD AT DUSK

A WOMAN'S BEAUTY IS LIKE A WHITE FRAIL BIRD

FROM: THE ONLY JEALOUSY OF EMER:

A PLAY

A WOMAN'S BEAUTY IS LIKE A WHITE
Frail bird, like a white sea-bird alone
At daybreak after stormy night
Between two furrows upon the ploughed land:
A sudden storm, and it was thrown
Between dark furrows upon the ploughed land.
How many centuries spent
The sedentary soul
In toils of measurement
Beyond eagle or mole,
Beyond hearing or seeing,
Or Archimedes' guess,
To raise into being
That loveliness?

A strange, unserviceable thing,
A fragile, exquisite, pale shell,
That the vast troubled waters bring
To the loud sands before day has broken.
The storm arose and suddenly fell
Amid the dark before day had broken.
What death? what discipline?
What bonds no man could unbind,
Being imagined within
The labyrinth of the mind,
What pursuing or fleeing,
What wounds, what bloody press,
Dragged into being
This loveliness?

A SUDDEN BLOW: THE GREAT WINGS BEATING STILL
Above the staggering girl, her thighs caressed
By the dark webs, her nape caught in his bill,
He holds her helpless breast upon his breast.

How can those terrified vague fingers push
The feathered glory from her loosening thighs?
And how can body, laid in that white rush,
But feel the strange heart beating where it lies?

A shudder in the loins engenders there
The broken wall, the burning roof and tower
And Agamemnon dead.
                              Being so caught up,
So mastered by the brute blood of the air,
Did she put on his knowledge with his power
Before the indifferent beak could let her drop?

Walter Frederick Osborne   EVENING

MY HOUSE

FROM: MEDITATIONS IN TIME OF CIVIL WAR

AN ANCIENT BRIDGE, AND A MORE ANCIENT TOWER,
A farmhouse that is sheltered by its wall,
An acre of stony ground,
Where the symbolic rose can break in flower,
Old ragged elms, old thorns innumerable,
The sound of the rain or sound
Of every wind that blows;
The stilted water-hen
Crossing stream again
Scared by the splashing of a dozen cows;

A winding stair, a chamber arched with stone,
A grey stone fireplace with an open hearth,
A candle and written page.
Il Penseroso's Platonist toiled on
In some like chamber, shadowing forth
How the daemonic rage
Imagined everything.
Benighted travellers
From markets and from fairs
Have seen his midnight candle glimmering.

Two men have founded here. A man-at-arms
Gathered a score of horse and spent his days
In this tumultuous spot,
Where through long wars and sudden night alarms
His dwindling score and he seemed castaways
Forgetting and forgot;
And I, that after me
My bodily heirs may find,
To exalt a lonely mind,
Befitting emblems of adversity.

TURNING AND TURNING IN THE WIDENING GYRE

The falcon cannot hear the falconer;

Things fall apart; the centre cannot hold;

Mere anarchy is loosed upon the world,

The blood-dimmed tide is loosed, and everywhere

The ceremony of innocence is drowned;

The best lack all conviction, while the worst

Are full of passionate intensity.

Surely some revelation is at hand;

Surely the Second Coming is at hand.

The Second Coming! Hardly are those words out

When a vast image out of *Spiritus Mundi*

Troubles my sight: somewhere in sands of the desert

A shape with lion body and the head of a man,

A gaze blank and pitiless as the sun,

Is moving its slow thighs, while all about it

Reel shadows of the indignant desert birds.

The darkness drops again; but now I know

That twenty centuries of stony sleep

Were vexed to nightmare by a rocking cradle,

And what rough beast, its hour come round at last,

Slouches towards Bethlehem to be born?

I

THAT IS NO COUNTRY FOR OLD MEN. THE YOUNG
In one another's arms, birds in the trees,
– Those dying generations – at their song,
The salmon-falls, the mackerel-crowded seas,
Fish, flesh, or fowl, commend all summer long
Whatever is begotten, born, and dies.
Caught in that sensual music all neglect
Monuments of unageing intellect.

II

An aged man is but a paltry thing,
A tattered coat upon a stick, unless
Soul clap its hands and sing, and louder sing
For every tatter in its mortal dress,
Nor is there singing school but studying
Monuments of its own magnificence;
And therefore I have sailed the seas and come
To the holy city of Byzantium.

III

O sages standing in God's holy fire
As in the gold mosaic of a wall,
Come from the holy fire, perne in a gyre,
And be the singing-masters of my soul.
Consume my heart away; sick with desire
And fastened to a dying animal
It knows not what it is; and gather me
Into the artifice of eternity.

IV

Once out of nature I shall never take
My bodily form from any natural thing,
But such a form as Grecian goldsmiths make
Of hammered gold and gold enamelling
To keep a drowsy Emperor awake;
Or set upon a golden bough to sing
To lords and ladies of Byzantium
Of what is past, or passing, or to come.

THROUGH WINTER-TIME WE CALL ON SPRING,

And through the spring on summer call,

And when abounding hedges ring

Declare that winter's best of all;

And after that there's nothing good

Because the spring-time has not come –

Nor know that what disturbs our blood

Is but its longing for the tomb.

R. Brassey Dunbar SPRINGTIME

Walter Frederick Osborne   THE RISING MOON, GALWAY HARBOUR

FIRST LOVE

FROM: A MAN YOUNG AND OLD

I

THOUGH NURTURED LIKE THE SAILING MOON

In beauty's murderous brood,
She walked awhile and blushed awhile
And on my pathway stood
Until I thought her body bore
A heart of flesh and blood.

But since I laid a hand thereon
And found a heart of stone
I have attempted many things
And not a thing is done,
For every hand is lunatic
That travels on the moon.

She smiled and that transfigured me
And left me but a lout,
Maundering here, and maundering there,
Emptier of thought
Than the heavenly circuit of its stars
When the moon sails out.

THE MERMAID

III

A MERMAID FOUND A SWIMMING LAD,

Picked him for her own,
Pressed her body to his body,
Laughed; and plunging down
Forgot in cruel happiness
That even lovers drown.

CRAZED THROUGH MUCH CHILD-BEARING
The moon is staggering in the sky;
Moon-struck by the despairing
Glances of her wandering eye
We grope, and grope in vain,
For children born of her pain.

Children dazed or dead!
When she in all her virginal pride
First trod on the mountain's head
What stir ran through the countryside
Where every foot obeyed her glance!
What manhood led the dance!

Fly-catchers of the moon,
Our hands are blenched, our fingers seem
But slender needles of bone;
Blenched by that malicious dream
They are spread wide that each
May rend what comes in reach.

THE NINETEENTH CENTURY AND AFTER

THOUGH THE GREAT SONG RETURN NO MORE
There's keen delight in what we have:
The rattle of pebbles on the shore
Under the receding wave.

John Atkinson Grimshaw WATCHING A MOONLIT LAKE

I MEDITATE UPON A SWALLOW'S FLIGHT,

Upon an aged woman and her house,

A sycamore and lime tree lost in night

Although that western cloud is luminous,

Great works constructed there in nature's spite

For scholars and for poets after us,

Thoughts long knitted into a single thought,

A dance-like glory that those walls begot.

There Hyde before he had beaten into prose

That noble blade the Muses buckled on,

There one that ruffled in a manly pose

For all his timid heart, there that slow man,

That meditative man, John Synge, and those

Impetuous men, Shawe-Taylor and Hugh Lane,

Found pride established in humility,

A scene well set and excellent company.

They came like swallows and like swallows went,

And yet a woman's powerful character

Could keep a swallow to its first intent;

And half a dozen in formation there,

That seemed to whirl upon a compass-point,

Found certainty upon the dreaming air,

The intellectual sweetness of those lines

That cut through time or cross it withershins.

Here, traveller, scholar, poet, take your stand

When all those rooms and passages are gone,

When nettles wave upon a shapeless mound

And saplings root among the broken stone,

And dedicate – eyes bent upon the ground,

Back turned upon the brightness of the sun

And all the sensuality of the shade –

A moment's memory to that laurelled head.

Charles Robertson BY THE RIVER

UNDER MY WINDOW-LEDGE THE WATERS RACE,

Otters below and moor-hens on the top,

Run for a mile undimmed in Heaven's face

Then darkening through 'dark' Raftery's 'cellar' drop,

Run underground, rise in a rocky place

In Coole demesne, and there to finish up

Spread to a lake and drop into a hole.

What's water but the generated soul?

Upon the border of that lake's a wood

Now all dry sticks under a wintry sun,

And in a copse of beeches there I stood,

For Nature's pulled her tragic buskin on

And all the rant's a mirror of my mood:

At sudden thunder of the mounting swan

I turned about and looked where branches break

The glittering reaches of the flooded lake.

Another emblem there! That stormy white

But seems a concentration of the sky;

And, like the soul, it sails into the sight

And in the morning's gone, no man knows why;

And is so lovely that it sets to right

What knowledge or its lack had set awry,

So arrogantly pure, a child might think

It can be murdered with a spot of ink.

Sound of a stick upon the floor, a sound

From somebody that toils from chair to chair;

Beloved books that famous hands have bound,

Old marble heads, old pictures everywhere;

Great rooms where travelled men and children found

Content or joy; a last inheritor

Where none has reigned that lacked a name and fame

Or out of folly into folly came.

Paul Jacob Naftel A WOODLAND GLADE

A spot whereon the founders lived and died
Seemed once more dear than life; ancestral trees
Or gardens rich in memory glorified
Marriages, alliances and families,
And every bride's ambition satisfied.
Where fashion or mere fantasy decrees
We shift about – all that great glory spent –
Like some poor Arab tribesman and his tent.

We were the last romantics – chose for theme
Traditional sanctity and loveliness;
Whatever's written in what poets name
The book of the people; whatever most can bless
The mind of man or elevate a rhyme;
But all is changed, that high horse riderless,
Though mounted in that saddle Homer rode
Where the swan drifts upon a darkening flood.

PARTING

FROM: A WOMAN YOUNG AND OLD

He. Dear, I must be gone
  While night shuts the eyes
  Of the household spies;
  That song announces dawn.
She. No, night's bird and love's
  Bids all true lovers rest,
  While his loud song reproves
  The murderous stealth of day.
He. Daylight already flies
  From mountain crest to crest.
She. That light is from the moon.
He. That bird . . .
She.   Let him sing on,
  I offer to love's play
  My dark declivities.

FROM: SUPERNATURAL SONGS

AS THE MOON SIDLES UP

Must she sidle up,
As trips the sacred moon
Away must she trip:
'His light had struck me blind
Dared I stop'.

She sings as the moon sings:
'I am I, am I;
The greater grows my light
The further that I fly'.
All creation shivers
With that sweet cry.

Walter Frederick Osborne CATTLE IN A MEADOW

PICTURE AND BOOK REMAIN,
An acre of green grass
For air and exercise,
Now strength of body goes;
Midnight, an old house
Where nothing stirs but a mouse.

My temptation is quiet.
Here at life's end
Neither loose imagination,
Nor the mill of the mind
Consuming its rag and bone,
Can make the truth known.

Grant me an old man's frenzy.
Myself must I remake
Till I am Timon and Lear
Or that William Blake
Who beat upon the wall
Till Truth obeyed his call;

A mind Michael Angelo knew
That can pierce the clouds
Or inspired by frenzy
Shake the dead in their shrouds;
Forgotten else by mankind,
An old man's eagle mind.

THE LOVER'S SONG

BIRD SIGHS FOR THE AIR,
Thought for I know not where,
For the womb the seed sighs.
Now sinks the same rest
On mind, on nest,
On straining thighs.

LONG-LEGGED FLY

THAT CIVILISATION MAY NOT SINK
Its great battle lost,
Quiet the dog, tether the pony
To a distant post.
Our master Caesar is in the tent
Where the maps are spread,
His eyes fixed upon nothing,
A hand under his head.

Like a long-legged fly upon the stream
His mind moves upon silence.

That the topless towers be burnt
And men recall that face,
Move most gently if move you must
In this lonely place.
She thinks, part woman, three parts a child,
That nobody looks; her feet
Practise a tinker shuffle
Picked up on the street.

Like a long-legged fly upon the stream
Her mind moves upon silence.

That girls at puberty may find
The first Adam in their thought,
Shut the door of the Pope's chapel,
Keep those children out.
There on that scaffolding reclines
Michael Angelo.
With no more sound than the mice make
His hand moves to and fro.

Like a long-legged fly upon the stream
His mind moves upon silence.

Say that the men of the old black tower,

Though they but feed as the goatherd feeds,

Their money spent, their wine gone sour,

Lack nothing that a soldier needs,

That all are oath-bound men:

Those banners come not in.

There in the tomb stand the dead upright,

But winds come up from the shore:

They shake when the winds roar,

Old bones upon the mountain shake.

Those banners come to bribe or threaten,

Or whisper that a man's a fool

Who, when his own right king's forgotten,

Cares what king sets up his rule.

If he died long ago

Why do you dread us so?

There in the tomb drops the faint moonlight,

But wind comes up from the shore:

They shake when the winds roar,

Old bones upon the mountain shake.

The tower's old cook that must climb and clamber

Catching small birds in the dew of the morn

When we hale men lie stretched in slumber

Swears that he hears the king's great horn.

But he's a lying hound:

Stand we on guard oath-bound!

There in the tomb the dark grows blacker,

But wind comes up from the shore:

They shake when the winds roar,

Old bones upon the mountain shake.

BECAUSE WE LOVE BARE HILLS AND STUNTED TREES
And were the last to choose the settled ground,
Its boredom of the desk or of the spade, because
So many years companioned by a hound,
Our voices carry; and though slumber-bound,
Some few half wake and half renew their choice,
Give tongue, proclaim their hidden name – 'Hound Voice.'

The woman that I picked spoke sweet and low
And yet gave tongue. 'Hound Voices' were they all.
We picked each other from afar and knew
What hour of terror comes to test the soul,
And in that terror's name obeyed the call,
And understood, what none have understood,
Those images that waken in the blood.

Some day we shall get up before the dawn
And find our ancient hounds before the door,
And wide awake know that the hunt is on;
Stumbling upon the blood-dark track once more,
Then stumbling to the kill beside the shore;
Then cleaning out and bandaging of wounds,
And chants of victory amid the encircling hounds.

Charles Thomas Burt WALKING UP

Acknowledgements

Bridgeman Art Library, *pages 20 and 39*

Bonhams, London/Bridgeman Art Library, *page 45*

Christie's Images, *pages 30, 58, 61, 62, 71, 95 and cover*

Christie's London/Bridgeman Art Library, *page 69*

Fine Art Society, London/Bridgeman Art Library, *page 19*

Guildford Borough Council/Bridgeman Art Library, *page 84*

Guildhall Art Gallery, Corporation of London/Bridgeman Art Library, *pages 43 and 66*

The Hugh Lane Municipal Gallery of Modern Art, Dublin, *pages 29 and 80*

Courtesy of The National Gallery of Ireland, Dublin, *pages 13, 40, 48, 52 and 57*

The Oriel Gallery, Dublin, *page 47*

Sotheby's, London, *pages 2, 6, 16, 23, 27, 35, 36, 65, 74, 79, 83 and 90*

Towneley Hall Art Gallery and Museum/Bridgeman Art Library, *page 51*

Christopher Wood Gallery, London/Bridgeman Art Library, *pages 54 and 87*

PICTURE RESEARCH: GABRIELLE ALLEN

*The author is grateful to Anne Yeats for her kind permission to reproduce the paintings by
Jack Butler Yeats on pages 2 and 6*

*The publishers have made every effort to trace the copyright-holders, but if they have
inadvertently overlooked any, they will be pleased to make the necessary arrangement at the
first opportunity. Despite all their efforts they have not been able to trace the copyright holder
for the painting on page 29.*